PUSHING YOUR BOUNDARIES:

A MEMOIR

One woman's journey through sport,
education, career, and travel.

BE OPEN TO POSSIBILITIES - say "YES!"

_"ONLY THOSE WHO WILL RISK GOING TOO FAR
CAN POSSIBLY FIND OUT HOW FAR ONE CAN
GO" - TS Elliot_

D1520087

By Dr. JERRI BARDEN PERKINS, MD '66

DEDICATION

For my mother Sybil Sullivan Barden, who empowered me as a child and my husband, John Calvin Perkins – or Cal as we called him. The love of my life, my best friend, mentor, and the man behind any successes achieved.

Contents

1. Introduction: THE BIKING CHALLENGE

When a friend of mine asked to bike 247 km through the Loire Valley Castle region in France, I could have said no and ended the conversation. Saying yes gave me time to ask myself some questions; why me, I am not a cyclist. The most I had ever achieved was a 25-mile ride. This trip required 25 *or more* miles a day for *six consecutive days*. It included traveling around all of the famous and breath-taking Loire Valley Castles. We were to start in Villandry to see the beautiful gardens, then the plan was to continue exploring the countryside from Chambord Castle and Blois. After that, on to the picturesque city of Amboise and then castles Chennonceau and Usse - among others. *Was I capable? Did I have time to train? Why would I consider this challenge?* Well, I have always loved learning and traveling so the answers to these questions seemed obvious. However, after more than a year without leaving my home following the Pandemic, and France one of my favorite cities filled with castles, croissants, and chocolates, how could I possibly say, "NO!"

And so, I did my research and reached out to my network of friends. I'm fortunate to have many friends who are younger and athletic! Each of them offered their assistance. Nancy, my first trainer, was a cyclist and gave guidance on how to prepare in 2 months. First step: get a baseline on your current biking ability. After a 2-year Pandemic, my skill the first day was only 6 miles. "Add 3 miles a week," she said. How this would work, I had no idea... But I trusted her. Why, she trains athletes for the Boston marathon!

My trainer, spin teacher, friends, and my son were all my team supporters. During training I fell twice on street crossings and called my son, who is a doctor. I was questioning my judgment. My son Jack encouraged me and said, "I will come down and personally put you on the plane!"

Training for the trip pressed me to do more physically than I thought possible. Yes, I could manage the biking but then I discovered that sitting and riding for many hours each day took a toll on my rear end! I called my dermatologist because the irritation was so severe that it caused bleeding. Solving this required over the counter medication and even more padding for my bottom. Without the support from my teachers, trainers, and family, I could not have achieved success followed by a gratifying feeling of empowerment.

I had originally envisioned this trip as a 5-star experience with guides and a van available to take me and my bike to the next hotel in case it rained or if I was too tired to finish the day's journey. The reality was that we went from town to town without a GPS, no cell reception, and only the 2 of us. Had anyone asked me prior to the Pandemic, I would not have considered such a trip!

We started on our bikes at 11 am daily and ended around 7 to 9 hours later. What an amazing trip; being lost, riding on the highway, in the pouring rain and <u>all the hills</u>!! I had the experience of a lifetime and learned more about myself and what I was capable of doing. Being open to possibilities allowed me to go farther than I had ever imagined. All you have to do is say YES!

2. <u>BEING RASIED IN THE SEGREGATED SOUTH IN THE 1950s</u>

Growing up in Richmond, VA, we were taught the importance of living in the Capital of the Confederacy. The historical significance of Virginia as one of the original colonies was a consistent lesson, as Virginia produced Presidents and amazing leaders like Thomas Jefferson. We were given little information on segregation or slavery. I loved the history and beauty of the city and felt fortunate to live there. At home and school, I was taught equality. Clearly at that time, it was not reality. Public restrooms were clearly marked "White Women Only." Although I do not recall asking why, I do remember that my mother told me the restrooms for black women were located elsewhere. Though I did not see other restrooms, I believed they did not wish to use the ones that I did see.

Monument Avenue was a beautiful tree-lined street with magnificent houses; once a favored living area for the city's upper class. It was originally lined with bronze statues representing and honoring those who fought for the Confederacy during the American Civil War. They were removed from their memorial pedestals in 2021.

Born in a charity hospital, I did not realize being white was a privilege. Certainly not anything that I felt. My family was as poor as a turkey! We lived in rented apartments with little (if any) heat. I was told that when I was a baby, the water glass beside our bed froze at night and my diapers were changed on newspaper on the floor. I was undernourished, anemic, and often suffered from respiratory illness. There were times that food was scarce because the money ran out and that was that. I know firsthand what it's like to be hungry and poor and cold.

As a young child we lived in what was called a "mixed" neighborhood. We always took public transportation as we had no car. We rode buses, trolleys, or walked. Buses were segregated. The significance of this separation escaped me then. I was a child and no one discussed it. It just existed and that's the way it was.

My mother, decades ahead of her time, encouraged education as my path forward. She was my advocate for higher education and having a career. She firmly believed that college was the key to success and so I believed that if I studied and worked, I could achieve my goals. She wanted me to attend a local college but I wanted to go away to school. I was determined to attend the best I could possibly afford, Mary Washington College – at the time, it was the girl's college of the University of Virginia — even entire schools were segregated into boys and girls! I am often told by friends and classmates how fortunate I was to have a mother who inspired and encouraged me. She worked as did I to achieve that goal. When she knew that she was dying, she apologized to me for pushing me so hard. I said, "I am grateful to you because I am very happy for the life I have and I am happy with the person I've become and I would not change that."

Not unlike segregation, my mother never mentioned that being a girl was a disadvantage in any way. I discovered this from my female classmates in college – they behaved as though their job was to take care of men.

In the 1950s, most teenage girls were not encouraged to have a college degree nor be independent. Most of my classmates were in college for their MRS – you might know this as the title for a married woman. Women went to college to find husbands, not to complete school and get a degree! Because Mary Washington College was a school for women only at the time, most of us dated guys from the University of Virginia or Quantico - the Marine Base close to our college. I remember that one of the upper classmates became pregnant and was asked to leave school. At the time, it was unacceptable to be in school while pregnant. Although I did not know her, I felt sad that she was not allowed to complete her education.

3. <u>BEING A WOMAN WAS TWO STRIKES AGAINST ME: NOT A DETERENT BUT A CHALLENGE</u>

My first job was a nurse's aide in a local Hospital in our hometown. All doctors in the hospital taking care of women and children were men. I was bold enough at 15 to believe I could do better for those patients and I set my goal on becoming a doctor. I believed that as a female doctor I could offer more and be more compassionate to the needs of female patients than the male doctors that I encountered. I understand that the majority of women today prefer a female over a male OB/GYN. And so, my goal was - and continues to be – to create a better world for women and children.

I recognized two immediate challenges: 1) discrimination against women in medicine and 2) funding. During my interview for medical school, I was told by the Dean that "I had 2 strikes against me." I realized that the first one is being female... but what is the second? His reply, "Being a woman IS two strikes against you".

There was no encouragement from anyone on my dream of medical school. Even my mother wanted me to accept a teaching scholarship instead. Mary Washington was considered an excellent college for girls as a part of the University of Virginia and the best education within my financial grasp. I made the Dean's List consistently, received a small - but meaningful - scholarship of one hundred dollars. (To put that into perspective, tuition for medical school at the time was five hundred dollars a year.) At Mary Washington I finally found positive support from 2 of my science professors. I began as a pre-med student and quickly realized that did not offer opportunities for summer jobs which were essential for funding my education.

A degree in chemistry offered more financial aid and met all necessary requirements for admission to medical school. Fortunately, those 2 professors trained at University of Virginia, were not graduating me without a liberal arts education for which I am grateful! More important than I realized when I entered the NIH world of the best and brightest. Science alone was not sufficient education when your colleagues are from the best and brightest of the Ivy League Schools. I needed to fit in with them. I knew I needed a broader and more balanced curriculum.

Early during our first year in medical school, we had one professor who lectured not on medicine but on confidence building. His story was simple. If you are in line to go to a movie, you should present yourself as a person of confidence and recognition, you would be recognized as a person of importance and told to proceed immediately to the front of the line. Whereas most of guys in my class clearly did not need to be told how important they were, it certainly was new to me. How wonderful it would be if all young women had that confidence – or a confidence building lesson - instilled early in life.

4. TOTAL FOCUS IN COLLEGE WAS ENTRANCE INTO MEDICAL SCHOOL

During the 1960s, it was not unusual for high school and college female
students to encounter discouraging and disapproving attitudes toward
females interested in going to medical school. While in college, I was told
that no one from Mary Washington has been accepted at the Medical College
of Virginia in 25 years. This was not a deterrent but a challenge for me.
The prevailing opinion was "women have no place going into medicine."
They will only take a spot away from a man, get married and never
practice. At that time female students made up only 10% of the class. Within the state of
Virginia for a female to be admitted to medical school, she had to be better than any in-state

male applicants – basically the best and brightest.

The first day in medical school, at the Medical College of Virginia, I was behind. Many of my classmates were in a better financial position than I was; meaning they were able purchase books in advance. I was struggling to afford to even buy the books as I got there! I did ultimately catch up with them and in doing so I learned that education is a journey and not a goal. Medical school was our life. There were neither vacations nor birthday parties. I worked Holidays and summers. On Saturday evenings I would join the guys in the Emergency Room to put in a few stitches from Saturday night fights. I knew some of the fellows were uncomfortable having a female classmate and very aware of the sex discrimination from the professors. There were no dressing rooms for female medical students as there were for men. I used the nurses' dressing quarters. Men ruled. That was it. Medical school also introduced me to racial and religious discrimination. There were two fraternities and no clubs for women. One for Jewish men and one for non-Jewish men. There was also a white hospital and a black hospital. In our last two years we saw patients in both. In the black hospital, we functioned as doctors. It was there that I delivered 25 babies in 30 days. Students in the white hospital were not even allowed to touch private paying patients. As you can imagine, this was not always in the best interests of the patients.

One evening I was working in obstetrics in the white hospital. My orders were clear from the private OB. "Stay with the patient but do nothing!" He then went to dinner at the local diner across the street. There were no cell phones or pagers back then and no instructions were left in case any problems arose. She was on a gurney and I was just to stand by and be there with her. Not long after he left, she was clearly ready to deliver. I could not check on her progress nor leave her side. Although I had not heard of nor trained in Lamaze breathing, I talked her through the pain with deep breathing. Her doctor finally returned and she was immediately taken to delivery but even as a student I still believed that being a woman, I was more sensitive to the needs of fellow women. I could do better. Is this the way I would have treated one of my female patients in labor?

Only when I reached medical school did I realize my dream of being an OB/GYN physician was not an option for me. Physically demanding for anyone but for me, being malnourished as a child, anemic from selling blood as a student, and sleep deprived from being on call, this was not a realistic goal. Fortunately, today the on-call shifts are not as lengthy and students aren't working themselves to the point of exhaustion. This makes it less difficult to handle the necessary physical demands of being an OB/GYN. So, there I was... I had studied for 4 years in college, then done 4 years of medical school and was about to receive my Doctorate of Medicine Degree, or MD. My dream of delivering babies was lost and I faced a humbling reality. And on top of that, I only weighed one hundred pounds. I just didn't have the stamina! *Ok, now what?*

5. <u>TRAINING ON THE HOSPITAL WARDS</u>

Our first two years were basic training in medical sciences. It was not until our third and fourth years that we trained in the Hospital Clinics or Wards. We all dressed professionally. Females wore white skirts, a blouse, and a white jacket with heels. Skirts had to cover your knees. This was the '60s! In surgery or the delivery rooms we wore surgical scrub *dresses.* Having limited funds, I bought two white outfits, skirts to the knee, and I hand monogramed my blouses to maintain my independence. What I did not realize was that my outfit was cotton and when they were washed for the first time, the skirts would shrink into a mini skirt. I had never seen a mini skirt before and was amazed that no comment was made by administration and certainly no objection by my male classmates. I found the nurses, especially the obstetric nurses where I delivered babies, most helpful. For my first delivery I turned to the nurse and said, "you have more experience here than I do." I acknowledged reality; it <u>was</u> my first delivery and I am confident she had witnessed many deliveries.

Our hospital, the Medical College of Virginia in Richmond, VA., was world renowned for having Dr. David Hume, who had the National Institute of Health (NIH) funding for research, therefore the Medical College was able to benefit. How fortunate I was training in a research center with Dr. Frank Mullinax as a mentor. He had NIH funding for research on RA, rheumatoid arthritis and obtained NIH training funding for me.   We published our work before graduation and I was offered an NIH Fellowship, unusual for a woman at the time. I had no idea this was generally reserved for the best and brightest physicians from Ivy League schools with years of training. My offer was in an Infectious Disease Laboratory though my dream was to continue my RA research. Dr. Mullinax said "Jerri, if offered an NIH Fellowship, take it. No matter what specialty." This is a possibility to which I was open – of course I said, "yes!"

I was fortunate enough to be friends with some of the guys in both fraternities and each had their own study notes from previous students passed down from year to year within the club. They generously shared with me. If there were any study binders passed among female students, I never saw one.

In discussions with classmates, I found that I was not only the youngest but also the most naïve. I thought that everyone went to medical school for the greater good! I went to medical school to make a difference, while some said they just went to make money.

The surgical research team was always roaming the halls looking for "end-of-life" patients for research purposes. Now, keep in mind that their research primarily involved utilizing organs for transplant. This is why I would stand in the doorway with my elbows out to block the way.

No matter the medical condition, I said that the patients are doing well. I was protecting people to the point that I may not have always been doing them a favor. I did not recognize quality of life as a consideration. I did my best to keep them alive as long as I could but... was that always in the best interest of the patient? I'm not entirely sure.

Older white doctors would not even allow our one black student to speak with his private patients. As one of my classmates said, "Jerri, these are not people, they are here for you to learn on." I was shocked and horrified to know how classmates felt about some patients. This was not how I was raised, nor how I planned to live my life.

Training on the wards our senior year, I found that sharing the good news on my NIH Fellowship was not well received. Students who interned in local hospitals were given an A or B for that month's rotation. I received a C. They favored those planning to practice medicine at any of the local hospitals. After a couple of rotations, I decided to consider the specialty of each month. Amazingly, I began receiving an A or B. For example; when asked what path I was considering, I would respond, "I'm considering Pediatrics or Psychiatry," because those were the specialties of that month's rotation. Therefore, I just kept doing that for each month! And so, up until I began to show an interest in the specialty of the month, I had received a C.

All female students were housed in a female dormitory that was not restricted to female medical students. Like my male classmates, I was sleep deprived after doing 36 hours of the same call schedule and work. Having a curfew was more than I was willing to accept. I rebelled. It was unreasonable for the women to have a curfew and nothing for the men. Though I don't clearly recall how I expressed my objections, I do vividly remember the result. Instead of limiting my call after midnight on a

Saturday, which was my original goal, I obtained new housing for all female medical students. A victory, yes, but not the one I had hoped!

I do recall an occasion when my male classmates called me in the middle of the night for help. A young woman without health insurance had become pregnant because she didn't have the funding for birth control. She had used a coat hanger to self-abort, and was clearly in medical distress. My classmates, asking me for help, "what do we do for this woman?" My answer was, "call an attending physician." Students are often reluctant to call an attending physician, which is a licensed doctor specializing in obstetrics, during middle of night. As students we had no training in dealing with this issue and if she was to survive, she needed an experienced doctor with appropriate training and not a student. I would do whatever necessary to save a patient — if the attending physician was upset to receive a late-night call, then that's too bad. I would make the call and was glad that my male classmates did so after calling me.

The attending came over and not only saved her life but saved her ability to have children in the future. My male classmates had called and asked me for help because I am a woman and they didn't know how to handle the situation. I did help them, and the woman was saved.

Although our School was known for its outstanding research, the Dean addressed the Junior class admonishing any graduate not practicing medicine. Before finishing my 3-year Fellowship at the NIH with numerous publications, Dr. Mullinax invited me to return and address the medical students in the amphitheater regarding my initial research. Later I rediscovered a micro-organism, first studied by Dr. Albert Sabin of the Sabin Vaccine, named for me in the American Tissue Type Collection.

6. AT THE NIH WE ALL DREAMED OF BEING A NOBEL LAUREATE!

Many at the NIH were Nobel Laureates. Medical school was competitive, cutthroat, but NIH was right in the heart, competitive!

Once again, I found myself challenged by the best and brightest Ivy Fellows. My first challenge was understanding their English. I was from the South and apparently had an accent. That's actually still a problem for me with London taxi drivers!

Dr. John Decker, Director of the Clinical Center at the NIH, was my mentor. He was dedicated to finding an inexpensive research model to study rheumatoid arthritis. At the time, a mycoplasma micro-organism was considered one possibility. He was collaborating with my Infectious Disease Lab and I was assigned to work with him and his team. Swine – or full-grown pigs - were the best model and an extremely expensive research tool. Our project involved mini pigs which weighed hundreds but were still very expensive.

We published several papers, and he offered me the opportunity of presenting at both domestic and international meetings - such an honor was traditionally reserved for the senior author, Dr. Decker.

Being the lone female Fellow on the NIH campus, it was hard to go unnoticed. Dr. Decker was well known, along with his research. When one of the white study rats in another research project at the Clinical Center developed arthritis, they called me. "We have a rat with arthritis, do you want to study it?" NO, I thought! I hate rats. But you guessed it, I said, "yes, I will be right over with my cage." In medical school I disliked studying living dogs and feeling the warm blood rushing through their blood vessels knowing that after the experiments, my lab partner would kill the animal. Although I did not like cutting the arthritic foot off the rat, it was easier than the dog experiments as I didn't witness the death of the animal. After studying, characterizing, and identifying the organism that caused arthritis in the rat as Mycoplasma pulmonis - the organism which caused the arthritis - I was given the honor of naming it. Thus, it was called "Mycoplasma pulmonis, jb strain." This was originally studied by Dr. Albert Sabin, and lost in the 1940s when he went off to War. The organism, jb strain, has been used by universities and available to other researchers in the American Tissue Type Collection. It is known to cause a Rheumatoid like arthritis in mice, a much more economical animal model – especially compared to swine and mini pigs.

7. <u>MARRIAGE WAS NOT MY DREAM BUT THE BEST DECISION I EVER MADE!</u>

NIH had a sailing club, and I <u>loved</u> sailing. A fact known to all who know me. Fortunately, one of the guys in the lab had a 27-foot mono-sail and was often looking for crew. Naturally, I volunteered. After a few years sailing, he asked me to marry him.

Of course, <u>I said yes</u> but really was uncertain that I would at the time. But if you say "no," then that ends the conversation! I discussed my concerns of marriage with other fellows at the NIH. I said, "I am afraid marriage might make me feel like a caged bird, not free." After a year, I married Cal – Dr. John Calvin Perkins, an avid sailor and skier, my best friend, mentor, and the best decision I ever made. There are several named scholarships in his memory at the University of Mary Washington. He already had 2 children - which we raised together - then we had another, and then we took a foster teen from Ethiopia into our home for a year. Being married and immediately having 2 children was without a doubt one of my biggest life challenges. They quickly learned the importance I placed on education. John, the younger of the two said to me, Lee his sister did not need to worry about that, "she would get married." I realized I had work ahead. I am now very proud to say that they are both educated and quite successful!

Although I can't remember when I stopped working prior to my delivery of Jack, I do recall that I planned to deliver a presentation in Europe two weeks after my due date. *What was I thinking?!* My due date passed and Jack was delivered by Cesarean Section. Instead of presenting as planned, I was out sailing with my 2-week-old son and family. I shared this story with Karen, Jack's wife, also a physician. She said, "No, Jerri, I am not impressed that Jack was sailing at 2 weeks old, but very impressed that you were sailing at 2 weeks post C-section!"

As the older children were leaving, why not consider taking in a foster child? Well, this was the time of famine with starving children of Ethiopia constantly in the news. We had room in our home, so why not? When I saw a flyer at our church requesting a home for one of these children, I said yes. Had I known he was a child soldier, would I still have said yes? I don't know. He was a bright well-mannered young man and I do not regret my decision. He was taken in by the nuns and brought into the U.S. by the Lutheran Church Services.   He had only 4 years of formal schooling and was now in our local high school in Montgomery County, Maryland - one of the best public schools in the state. Our son Jack referred to him as his brother.

To my surprise, I found that not all of my neighbors shared my feeling of welcome. One day he arrived home late from school, and I asked him why he was late.

[Him]: I went home with a classmate to study.

[Me]: Was it with a girl?

[Him]: Yes.

[Me]: Were her parents home?

[Him]: No.

[Me]: You shouldn't go home with a girl without her parents around.

[Him]: Why?

[Me]: Have you read *To Kill a Mockingbird*?

[Him]: Yes.

[Me]: That's the reason.

[Him]: That's not how it is anymore.

I was very aware that my neighbors didn't share my feelings of welcome, however he definitely was not. This prejudice I would have expected elsewhere but not in my neighborhood. Thankfully, the teachers at our neighborhood school were more welcoming and they volunteered to tutor him after school for hours each day. I tried to get him into a private school in the district and they would gladly accept him, but he did not have the background to succeed and believed he would do better in our school system. He was very bright, excellent at math, but government and compositions were challenging. He wished to share his knowledge and even taught Jack some Arabic!

As foster parents, we were given a small sum for his care. We put the money in a savings account for his college education. After graduating high school, he joined an Ethiopian band in Washington D.C. I said I would like to come and hear him play. His response was clear and emphatic, "NO!" He didn't tell me directly, but I understood that he was protecting me – as he always was. He then asked if he could have his college fund rather than use it for college. Of course, I gave it to him. Years later, he called on Thanksgiving and told me how sorry he was that he was a disappointment to me. He knew the importance I placed on education and he chose not to use the money that Cal and I put away for his schooling as we had originally intended. "Why? I am not disappointed. I want you to be happy in whatever career you choose," I said.

Raising children and working is challenging. With my new family, I wanted to be a full-time mom and only work part-time. Therefore, I negotiated a part time position at the NIH which disappeared in one of the many government budget cuts before I was able to return to work. *Now what?!*

Government is the industry in the DC area. I knew the FDA was hiring but had no idea what the FDA did. I was hired as a consultant 10 hours a week. My goal was always to return to my NIH research.

8. <u>NAVIGATING LIFE AS A WORKING MOM</u>

The FDA, or "The Agency" as we called it, hired me because of my training in Infectious Diseases at the National Institutes of Health. I was delighted to find a job working 10 hours a week and grateful for any additional funding for our household as a working mom. At that time, medical devices were not regulated, but drugs and other products were. The decision to begin this regulation was very much influenced by the fact that people were losing their sight after having lenses implanted into their eyes. Physicians could even make hip replacements in their home garages! Regulation was also new to medical device manufacturers. They were obviously concerned about this new regulation. The manufacturers expressed their concern by saying things like, "I feel like we're on the Titanic and the music is playing." Congressional hearings were ongoing. It was a very tumultuous time for the device industry.

This time, *I* was the challenge for the FDA. Having been trained in medical research at the NIH – where animal trials generally preceded human trials for other marketed pharmaceuticals like drugs and vaccines – this was not the case for these devices. At the FDA Advisory Panel meeting with the best eye experts in the country, I posed the question - how can you allow plastic to be implanted in eyes without any animal research studies?

Ultimately, I worked alongside the best and brightest in their fields once I learned that marketed products and research studies have different endpoints and goals. To be successful, it is essential to see both sides on any issue.

Shortly after arriving at the FDA, I was audited. I don't recall why there was an audit but for me, it was a good thing. The auditor came to my desk and asked to see the projects I was assigned. At the conclusion of my audit, she told me to find someone that will offer me a higher rank and she said, "you are producing well above your pay grade!" While I was simply pleased to have a part time job in the field that I loved, I ultimately did move from the Ophthalmic to the Orthopedic Division and became the Acting Division Director when the boss was away. This granted me the higher rank that the auditor had suggested.

The FDA issues regulations to ensure that drugs are safe and effective and to ensure that medical devices are reasonably safe and effective. As the medical expert on this issue, I was assigned to work with one of the lawyers on the regulations for these devices. The lawyer made sexual and threatening comments which I reported to my superiors. Their response was to remove me from the project and I was instructed to stay away from him. Having experienced numerous challenges, this was perhaps the most difficult for me. I felt punished for his error in judgment as I was the one removed from the project and yet he was allowed to remain. What now?

I read a Notice that The Office of the Commissioner was recruiting a Medical Officer. The requirements to apply were impressive. I went to a fellow Medical Officer and said I would like to apply but I am not sure that I qualify. His response, "Jerri, you are as qualified as anyone." Not only did I get the appointment but in an incredible coup, the full-time position listed was made into a part-time slot to accommodate me. It was an incredibly easy and smooth transition. Being open to possibilities afforded me this position.

My first high profile case was related to toxic shock syndrome. A tampon manufacturer mailed samples to many households across the country as part of a mass marketing campaign. Suddenly young women were dying from Toxic Shock, a bacterial infection believed to be related to the product. One of my assignments involved writing letters to physicians from the Office of the Commissioner to alert them on this deadly potential. In addition, I was interviewed on the radio and sent to a local TV station in Washington, D.C. for a live in person interview. *Wow*, I was so excited to be selected to discuss this important topic and proud of the work FDA was doing to keep women safe! The morning of the broadcast, I clearly remember sitting in my car outside the studio and realizing I had been sent in sacrifice. I was the only woman they had in the Office of the Commissioner. Had I ever heard anyone say a good word for our FDA? Not really. I was about to be publicly destroyed and I knew it. This was to be a point, counter-point discussion and I had no idea with whom I would be opposed. Then, to my surprise and delight, there stood the doctor who delivered my son. I was to engage in this discussion with him! I *loved* him! For television and the Hostess, it must have been the most boring and painful hour in history. He and I agreed on every medical and scientific point while the Hostess desperately expected controversy. She would continue to push an issue but since we already agreed with each other, it didn't go any further than that. I almost felt sorry for her! Ultimately, during my career I was given media training by the industry I represented for TV appearances which never aired. But the videos had been filmed and were ready to go, and I was now trained and prepared for the future!

One of my assignments in the office of the commissioner was to read CDC reports when I found the data linking aspirin to Reye Syndrome. Being a mom with a young child at home, I believed every mother should know what I knew. With data in hand, I wrote my recommendations to the Commissioner. Instead of a, "good job, Jerri," all work assignments were taken away and I was informed, "you might be happier in another position." This is really because there was no cause for termination so basically, I sat there and got paid. There was no work given to me at all.

At this level, I discovered politics and science sometimes clash. It is not easy to fire a government employee, but it is possible to take away all work assignments. Having experienced discrimination in medical school, working with the best and brightest in science - and now confronted with politics - *would I survive this challenge?*

It took the FDA 8 years, and another presidential election before acting on the association of aspirin and Reye Syndrome. This is a syndrome that occurs most often in children under fifteen years of age in which a rare disease damages the brain and liver causing death if not treated. Fortunately, Surgeon General, C. Everett Koop, notified the public 8 years earlier when he became aware of the issue. I can only imagine, as a mother, what I would have done had this not been the case.

I knew the FDA was always in need of Medical Officers and while working in the Office of the Commissioner, I had worked with several of the Division Directors. Dr. Merle Gibson was the Director of Division of Anti-Infective Drugs. I walked downstairs to his office and asked, "need another medical officer?" "Come on down," was his reply. Had he not retired less than 2 years after I arrived, I would have worked with him forever. We worked very well together. Although still part time, he assigned me to represent the FDA at one of the Advisory Panels where recommendations are made by experts whether a product should be approved for marketing. At the lower level within the Agency, science has more power than politics, but it does not always prevail.

At the time, assignments on anti-infective products were random. Since I was a part time medical officer, my products were generally not high priority. However, during the AIDS epidemic of the 1980s, I was given one that I believed was approvable. I then recommended the first AIDS related drug to receive FDA approval.

The government has some funding for professionals to go to medical meetings so that we can keep up with our education. It's hard enough to receive money for a full-time person to travel, let alone a part time person. The only way I could go was at my own expense. There are always new findings in the medical field and education is something I highly value. This is why I funded it myself. I made sure to attend all medical meetings that I could and ultimately presented at one of the International AIDS Conferences.

Working moms are also raising children and attending school functions. Jack, our youngest, was put in private schools to accommodate my schedule. In high school, he attended a private school in Washington, D.C. This all-boys school was a challenge for me. Being a mother, I was called upon to sponsor a tea for the school. "No," I said, "I don't do tea, I do donations." They certainly didn't call upon the fathers to sponsor tea. During one of the parents' dinners, I was seated next to a well-known writer for the Washington Post. Of course, I knew who he was. Seated next to him for the evening, what could we possibly have in common? Our sons. I began to tell him of my disappointment in Jack's lack of interest in his studies. His response was, "I was not a great student in high school, but I turned out alright." Yes, I was amused but more importantly, I relaxed during the meal and relaxed my thinking about my son's education. Yes, Jack turned out just fine as well.

A less amusing story from school was an investment with another one of Jack's classmates' parents. Cal was approached to invest in one of this parent's many companies. The money invested was to be repaid monthly in dividends within a year. Now, that sounds too good to be true - and it was. I was skeptical but agreed to the investment. First couple of months the dividend checks arrived. Things appeared to be going well. Suddenly the monthly checks stopped. Since this was Cal's investment, I was on his case to discuss the lack of dividends for months with the parent. This was not easy for Cal. He could not believe we had been swindled by a fellow private school parent. I picked up the phone when the father had called. He asked to speak with Cal. I let him know that I was aware of the issue and that we wanted our money returned. His response to me was, "You are a woman, this is a discussion for men and I want to speak with your husband." I asked him if he wanted me to go public with this. And I meant it. Our funds were promptly returned. Unfortunately, one of the professors called me for advice because he too had invested his entire retirement account with this same parent but for him, it was too late. The parent was indicted and his picture was plastered on the front page of the Metro section of the Washington Post as he was in hand cuffs and off to serve jail time for his scheme. My friends were surprised I didn't punch him for speaking to me that way!

9. <u>MY NEW CONSULTING CAREER: PERKINS AND PERKINS, INC</u>

Eight years prior to establishing my consulting firm, I first became a medical officer in medical devices. I had moved onto the Office of the Commissioner and finally became a reviewing medical officer for pharmaceutical products. During that time, I sat across the table with consultants that were obviously not trained in the field and were not qualified to serve the companies or patients they were working with. These consultants - and they were always men as I had never seen a female consultant - came to present their cases to the government in an effort to obtain approval from the FDA. What they often neglected to do was listen. The FDA makes the rules. It is their game and responsibility. Companies and consultants need to listen to what is needed and expected for regulatory approval, the goal. As a consultant I encouraged companies to assign one person, particularly at in-person meetings just to listen for FDA concerns. If industry representatives and consultants are meeting with the FDA just to present their case, they may lose. It is essential to *listen* and hear *why* the Agency has concerns and what data will be required to resolve the issue with a successful outcome. The challenge is having the FDA, say yes to approval. Consultants need to listen and, you guessed it, be open to possibilities.

I reviewed numerous products, some worthy of approval but not approved. I believed more products could and should be approved for patients with better understanding of what was required for approval by the pharmaceutical and medical device companies. Having been trained by the NIH and the FDA, I was in a position to help.

In the mid-1980s when I left the FDA, AIDS was an epidemic and a controversial topic which continues today in some countries of the world. Initially, latex condoms and gloves were the only available protection against the disease. It was again the Surgeon General, who invited those manufacturers into his office and said, "I am about to change your lives." These products previously required minimum regulation and they were suddenly high priority and lifesaving.

Upon starting my own consulting firm, I was advised that it is important to have at least 2 years' income saved up at the start of your new company. Those early years will let you know if you will succeed. I needed basic home office supplies, legal advice, and support from Cal - which I received in abundance. Every January was consistently slow, and felt that I had no idea if I would make it! After serval successful years, Cal finally said, "you say that every year." After that, I never said it again! The first few years I did do very well as I had just left the Agency and companies already knew me. They hired me without asking my fee.

I had no idea on marketing which is necessary to open a company and hire other consultants.

Where to begin? I contacted my lawyer as I had questions starting up. I was advised to send out flyers, which I thought was ridiculous but I was open to all ideas - and then it worked! I consulted on both condoms and gloves and I attended AIDS Conferences with Cal, who saw patients in his office and in the hospital while offering the clinical perspective to our company.

The AIDS Activists demanded action with their chants: "AIDS EQUALS DEATH!" They changed the FDA and regulated products forever with their passion and activism. Others definitely learned how to make a difference from those activists as women could also be seen chanting: "WE'RE DYING TOO!" We still see this passion and activism with breast cancer and other widespread medical concerns.

Cal and I both volunteered in a free clinic in Washington, D. C., which served the underserved and working poor. Some of our clients were college students with no money for antibiotics and no health insurance. They were working but they didn't have insurance, it was much less common at that time. Also, you could hear bullets in the nearby streets when the windows were open.

Not only did I see patients in the free clinic, but I also served 2 terms on their board. For the board meetings I drove down into DC by myself in my little red convertible sports car. As I approached the neighborhood, reality hit me. Was I going to park my car here at night alone?! I confess that I drove around the block, mustered my courage, and parked in the clinic lot. Yes, I made it. What I did not realize at that first board meeting was that my car and I could not have been safer anywhere. The neighborhood knew we were there to serve, we had no controlled substances and truly protected the volunteers! All we carried were antibiotics and things that had no value on the streets. It was difficult for me to serve on the board because I didn't prefer the administrative issues, however my contribution was that I knew the industry and was able to get the donations of condoms, gloves, and pharmaceuticals. Again, I am glad that I said "yes" even though I was primarily there for patient care. All I wanted to do was to see patients and help people.

I clearly remember one lovely young black female that I saw for infection related to IV drug abuse and gave my usual AIDS lecture. A few years later, she returned with the disease and specifically asked for me. She no longer looked young and beautiful, instead she looked skeletal, emaciated and dying. She said, "I wish I had listened." My heart was broken. While I enjoyed seeing patients, once they had the disease, I could offer little.

We did a study on the importance of educating the medical staff on infection control for this new deadly disease. During one of the International AIDS conferences, we presented our findings - which showed the education of staff was critical for safety. It was because of our AIDS research that Cal and I were invited to join other conference attendees in Stockholm, Sweden for cocktails with the King. I was thrilled to be at an outdoor event on the water's edge at the City Hall, where the Nobel Prize for Medicine is given. I may not get one, but I was there!

Cal served as my balance in family and career. He was now in private practice in Washington, D.C. and a member of the board and Chair of Infectious Diseases at one of the local hospitals. Because of his serving on the board and the chair, he received an invitation to all inaugural activities of President Bush. He handed me the invitation and said he had no interest. "This is a historic event, and we will attend," I replied. I invited a few executives from pharmaceutical and medical device companies and purchased a box at the ball.

One of the couples that I invited were immigrants to the U. S. and thrilled at the opportunity; another couple from the NIH and executives from big pharma who asked, "how are you getting there?" Not having a clue on protocol, I replied, "driving." He then provided two limos for our group. Not only was this practical, as there is no normal parking at this type of function, but also a luxurious treat!

Since Cal had no interest, it fell to me to appear in person with his invitation in Washington, D.C. to get the tickets. When I presented myself with his invitation, I was asked if I was "Mrs. Perkins." My typical response to this question was "NO, I am Dr. Jerri Barden Perkins," but his tickets could *only* be obtained in person by his wife with proper identification. So, on this occasion, I said, "yes!" What if I had said no?!

In the 1990s Bill Clinton became President and changed FDA rules. This was a major contribution to children and older adults. Being a working mom while at the FDA, I realized that most studies for FDA approval in medical devices and pharmaceuticals were studied in men. Dosages were determined by male subjects in studies, not in women and not in children.

President Clinton initiated what was called the "Pediatric Rule." Companies would now be required to study appropriate dosages for drugs used in children. Previously, doctors and parents had been guessing at what was appropriate for a child. Amazingly this had not been required earlier. With these new rules being established in the U.S., as a former FDA employee, I was invited to speak in London. Initially I was skeptical as I was no longer an insider at the Agency and uncertain that I would have access to the necessary requirements. I said yes and found that the FDA was anxious to educate companies and helpful to me in spreading FDA expectations. Companies were not prepared and never eager for new requirements. For 10 years I was invited to present on this New Rule from FDA and other regulatory requirements at International Conferences. I found it rewarding to know that attendees outside U. S. thought our FDA the Gold Standard for drug approval. That is not always the case here.

It was not unusual for me to be invited to speak on requirements for clinical trials used for regulatory approval. Perhaps the most meaningful to me was the Annual Fall Conference for the ACRP (the Association of Clinical Research Professionals) where the Keynote speaker was a Holocaust Survivor. She was a twin in one of Dr. Josef Mengele's studies at Auschwitz. Her stories from that experience literally brought tears running down my cheeks. Although I have never seen a presenter cry, I could not hold back after hearing her personal experiences. When she announced that she thought Dr. Mengele was a good researcher and she forgave her parents, I could not believe my ears. I was going to present and there I was in tears! After her, there was a presentation on the Nuremburg Trials. Again, I was left in tears. Fortunately, there was a coffee break before I spoke but what a challenge to follow those presentations. My job was to educate the audience on current requirements for clinical trials submitted to the FDA. I shall never forget my opening line, "Knowledge and discovery are often born out of tragedies."

Did you know that the FDA's Code of Federal Regulations is based on the Nuremburg Code? No person can be in a research study without their consent - that's the number one thing in the Nuremburg Code. Note that was not required until the 1970's! When I began auditing clinical trials consent was the number one issue. Today, it is no longer number one but remains a concern in some other countries.

My research at the NIH and my FDA training, which offered me a career in private consulting on clinical trials and allowing me to lecture and audit clinical studies all over the world, has given me the greatest satisfaction in life. It was important to me to ensure that patients are protected; that research studies are meaningful, and no patients are enrolled in studies without their consent. It truly gave me a reason to wake up in the morning. I loved what I did and I would be doing it to this day if I could. It gave me a real purpose in life – to be sure that people are protected.

10. <u>THE BIGGEST CHALLENGE: LOOSING THE LOVE OF MY LIFE</u>

If anyone had asked me what the biggest challenge in life was prior to Cal's death, I would have said raising children. Cal was diagnosed with Polycythemia vera, a type of cancer, and he lived with it for fourteen years. He never acknowledged his cancer and initially refused to tell his children. On this I would not yield. They must be informed. He did but believed he had another 10 years to live. How do I know? I was there when he told his End-of-Life Counselor.

How did we decide on an end-of-life psychiatrist? Cal was able to practice for many years but ultimately, he became too weak with bi-monthly transfusions. I was putting in more and more consulting hours, which I loved but it was exhausting being both breadwinner and care giver. Now I was doing the driving and dropping him off at the store or museum. One cold and windy afternoon I dropped him off at one of the Smithsonian museums in DC while I looked for parking and walking a mile back with the cold wind in my face. Now keep in mind that I have never been a fan of cold weather. "Cal," I said, "why not get a handicap pass for the car?" I knew he qualified, and it would make my life much easier. "NO," he said, "that is for those who need it." Yet another sign of his denial. But I needed help and told Cal that we should talk to someone. So, he turned to friends and found us a counselor. I walked into the office with the goal to have a handicap sticker for the car. To my surprise, our initial conversation was all about how to end Cal's life either by his hand or abroad. I was sitting there in total disbelief! This was an end-of-life psychiatrist. We finally approached the subject of the sticker. "Cal," he said, "I know you love Jerri and would do anything for her." "Of course," Cal responded. "It would really help her if you would get this sticker for her." "Yes," was his immediate response. Finally, I got my "yes" but did I really need therapy for this? The answer for me was again, "yes," and what a good lesson on communication with a loved one. He refused to say that he had cancer. He would always say that he had Polycythemia vera. He <u>never</u> said, "cancer." My challenge was acknowledging reality and allowing him to live his life in denial. I took a day to cry alone, made the decision I would accept whatever challenges and allow him to live life on his terms. We had trips planned to New York City that fell on the day he died and then another trip to Paris was planned for the following week. My son, Jack, said, "Mom, aren't you glad you did not go to Paris?" "No," I replied. "Cal would love to have one more croissant and coffee there!"

11. <u>TRAVEL WILL CHANGE YOUR LIFE</u>

Consulting on clinical trials afforded me the opportunity to travel in the U.S. and Europe. My dream had always been to see the pyramids of Egypt. Therefore, when the opportunity presented itself, <u>I said yes!</u> Cal said no, because it is too dangerous a country. After leaving the Agency, I engaged a speech writer to help me. First lesson, "what does your audience want to know." Giving these talks while at the NIH or the FDA, your audience listened because they wanted to learn current Agency thinking. I only wish I had acted earlier.

My speech writer was going to Egypt to visit her friends while staying at the U.S. Embassy, the U.S. Ambassador and his wife. This was by far the most fortified Embassy in the world at that time. When Cal said "no," I responded, "Never will we be safer." And off we went!

Our trip was arranged in part with the help of the Embassy friends. The month selected was March as desirable temperatures in 2001, only a few months before the 9/11.

Starting in Cairo, we visited the museum where the Rosetta Stone is a copy as the original resides in the British Museum in London. The mummy room was strikingly different from that in the British Museum, where you find large crowds, and noisy visitors packed to look at numerous preserved bodies. Here you walk into a solemn place; a small room with few visitors, silence, and respect for the dead. There was no talking allowed. It was a more spiritual setting. Our guide was outside the room for any questions.

Once we had breakfast with the ambassador's wife, then enjoyed lunch at the Four Seasons Hotel overlooking the Pyramids of Giza, and later we sailed the Nile. It was an amazing and unique experience that we would not have had without that yes to the opportunity.

Cal and I stayed in a nearby hotel and walked the streets alone. Strangers would come up and say, "American, we like Americans but not your government." It amazed us that people on the streets distinguished between an entire people and their government. A lesson for all of us!

When Jack was in college, there was a Study Abroad Program for students to study for a semester in Europe. His junior year, he asked to study in Parma, Italy. While Cal was at Exeter, he studied in France. I thought it was a wonderful experience that I had not enjoyed. Yes, I said. Cal said no. He said it was a "boondoggle." At the time, Cal didn't see the value in sending Jack to study abroad. Jack went, and then was offered to return and teach in their Italian program. This program offered him more of a learning experience than he could have gained in all semesters in his California college. Cal recognized the benefit and acknowledged it was the best maturing experience for Jack. The first scholarship I established in memory of Cal, was Travel Abroad. What a joy to know that we have already sent several students abroad to study!

Let this be a warning to Skiers from Zermatt to Italy for the day: take your toothbrush and passport. If you miss the last gondola at 3pm, you must stay the night in Italy! We missed the last gondola but managed to return safely the same night with the working crew. Cal and I both loved sailing and skiing. Our next trip included an avalanche. We were greeted at the train station by a horse drawn sleigh from the Grand Hotel Zermatterhof. A day late for our week's stay due to a friend's wedding, we were delighted to return and hit the slopes. Overnight, an avalanche buried the town and all power to hotels and lifts was halted. Staying in a 5 Star Hotel in an avalanche truly is charming with candle lights and gas heat for warmth and cooking. A lovely romantic setting to be sure but it only left us with 4 days of skiing as opposed to the original plan of 7 days. It was the most gorgeous and stunning place in the world – but I was there to ski! Finally, the power returned. Almost out the door, I heard a loud knock! "You must move to another room," said the head housekeeper. "No," I replied. She persisted - as did I. Cal said, "Jerri, let's just look at the other room." Reluctantly, I agreed. We followed her to an undisclosed part of the hotel. At the top, she opened the door into a luxury apartment. We entered the living room and saw a fireplace, a jacuzzi bath, then a bedroom with a second fireplace, and a dining room with two balconies overlooking the Matterhorn. *Wow.* "You may move us," I said.

Want to ski with your adult son? Invite him to go powder-cat skiing with you! If he loves to ski, he will say, "Yes!" First, you need to know it is described as "advanced for expert skiers who may encounter un-groomed black diamond runs in any condition with no groomed terrains."

There was only one other female on this adventure without training, or proper skis, who could not read the unmarked terrain. She had fallen and was transported by ambulance to the hospital. She refused the offer of powder skis! Because of this mishap, our trip was cut short but the smile on Jack's face at the top of Aspen, CO was worth a million!

Once Jack entered medical school, he wanted to join his classmates training in Africa. Since Cal, Jack, Jack's wife Karen, and I were all physicians, he wanted the four of us to travel to Africa and practice together. *What a great idea!* However, when the time arrived 4 years later, Cal was too ill, and I was working more to pay his medical expenses. Our compromise was to take the final week of Jack's training and join them for a week on Safari. In December, the date was set for the month of March. In the middle of February, Jack called. "Mom, how would you feel about moving the date to

May?" "No," I replied. "Let me confirm *your* reasons for going later. Going in March would require you only to observe and be paid a stipend. Your air fare and housing expenses covered, and academic credit fulfilled, correct?" His said, "well, when you put it like that it doesn't sound like a bad idea." As a result he did far more than observe, which was his concern. He became an expert in chest tube insertion, had a fantastic learning experience, and we all enjoyed our Safari. I handled this the in the same way I did when working at the FDA – to illustrate the other side of the coin. Then Jack said, "yes!"

I've worked in Paris, Rome, India, China, Japan and ultimately traveled with Cal around the world. Where he could see the beauty, I focused on the poverty of many of the poorer countries. While in Nepal traveling with the Harvard Alumni, as that was Cal's alma mater, I was appalled to learn that girls were not offered any education.

When I returned to the States, I organized a small group of my yoga friends and we each agreed to fund an education for 8 girls. Our Around the World lecturer from Notre Dame had visited schools while in Nepal so I reached out to him on how to make this happen. Sad to say, this one is not a success story. He informed me that the religious education network he knew there did not educate girls! When I learned that the University of Mary Washington Classics students were traveling to Nepal, I immediately offered funding support for a student. If I couldn't help 8 girls in Nepal, then I can help at least one student travel there in pursuit of education.

After Cal's death, I continued to travel with the Harvard group. They offered a trip to Rome with a Harvard professor who wrote a book dedicated to Pope Francis. The topic of the tour was an "Insider's Guide to Rome." I said, "yes, I love Rome. I worked there and visited several times with family but never had an official tour." During the Harvard professor's first lecture in Rome, he asked if anyone of the 10 of us traveling with him wanted to join him when he met Pope Francis? My hand was up immediately, "yes, I said!" No one else expressed an interest. The meeting was at the end of the trip and our group was scheduled to visit the Sistine Chapel on that day. I had seen the Chapel once before and once after the cleaning. Had I not, I believe I would still have said yes. At the next lecture the professor repeated, "does anyone wish to join me meeting Pope Francis?" Again, I said, "yes!" It was apparent I was the only one interested in joining the professor.

One of the other attendees pulled me aside and asked, "do you have a black dress?" "No." "Do you have something black for your head?" "No." Clearly, I was not concerned with following proper protocol attire. The Harvard professor and I had a very early breakfast and taxied to Vatican City for our meeting.

This was not his first visit. I was asked to have a seat and wait while he met with his contacts who were priests. They came out and we all proceeded through multiple layers of security. I did not utter a word, I just followed along. Finally, we arrived in St. Peter's Square on the podium with other dignitaries. The Pope greeted the thousands in his Pope mobile while I sat and wondered, *why me?* I did not belong there. *What had I done to deserve this honor?*

I studied, worked, graduated medical school, and vowed never to marry a doctor, especially one from Harvard who had no idea what an MRS degree was but "did not believe Harvard had one." None of this would have been possible if I hadn't been educated and married Cal. Being open to possibilities has enhanced my life and when invited to meet the Pope, I said yes! Although I felt unworthy, I was grateful to be there.

My expectation was only to watch the Harvard professor present his book to His Holiness. Imagine my surprise, when I was marched up by security to meet His Holiness, shake his hand and be given a treasured white rosary. Life is full of surprises when you are <u>open to possibilities</u>!

Travel has always been special for me. After paying off my government loans, my first trip was one that I found from a notice on the bulletin boards at the NIH. It was to Las Vegas, California, and Hawaii. I got to go to all of those places for a minimum amount of money and shared a room with a woman that I didn't know – and I didn't even care! I loved the incredible sights and the educational experiences. Having written many travel stories for my grandchildren, one of them, Devon, asked what is the poorest country I ever visited? For this I had no answer. I could name many places we traveled. I could not overlook the poverty in the world. After returning from our trip around the world, I remember commenting to one of our patients in the free clinic that we have not seen such poverty here. I actually thought, *"Did I say that to one of our patients? Yes."* And he agreed with me! We see poverty here and, on the news, but it is quite different to see firsthand children with swollen bellies from lack of protein and open fires in the streets with people living in tents. If I had my way, it would be mandatory for every American to study outside the US. It is so important to see how other people live. I truly believe education is best learned by living adventures.

12. <u>2019 A SPECIAL YEAR: THE DISTINGUISHED ALUMNI AWARD</u>

My classmate, Sylvia, nominated me for the University of Mary Washington's Distinguished Alumni Award. Three years earlier, I received pages of documents to be completed by me explaining why I should receive this honor. *Why me?* I did not know how to respond. I confess, I did not put my best effort into completing the documents as I felt undeserving. A second nomination the following year. I was more thoughtful but again I confess, it was not yet my best effort. I believed others were more deserving. Then I received a third nomination from Sylvia. I realized I should do my best to fulfill this request because she believed that I was worthy. Sylvia was persistent. It took 3 years before <u>I finally said yes</u>! This time I put everything I felt mentionable into the documents. That was the final year before the pandemic, and I was honored with the <u>Distinguished Alumni Award 2019.</u> If you fill out the paperwork and give it everything you've got, then who knows? Maybe you *are* worthy. Once again, being open to possibilities can surprise you in positive ways.

I know that many of us - especially women - feel unworthy. Since most of my mentors were men, they were less likely to acknowledge this. I don't have any data so I could be wrong but I think that women tend to not feel deserving. Is this a generational or a gender difference? I'm not sure.

Cal had given me a Grecian amphora, which I treasured. To put it into perspective, this amphora is listed in a museum in Rhodes, Greece. I told our son Jack, "Someday this will belong to you." His reply stunned me. "No thanks," he said. This inspired me to find a good home for my antiquity. Cal had encouraged me to donate to my university as Harvard was already well endowed. Then after Cal's death, I had reconnected with my university.

I placed a cold call to the University of Mary Washington (UMW) and said that I would like to donate my amphora. They returned my call and said, "yes!" However, as an antiquity transported into the U.S., they needed to authenticate it before they could accept the donation and it took a full year to do so. It gives me great joy to see my art displayed for students to study, knowing that someday, they will also enjoy the beauty of my authentic Greek Amphora that dates back to 200 BC.

Since then, I have donated other artworks to the University of Mary Washington Classics Department and funded several scholarships in memory of Cal. For ten years, I devoted my time to working and to funding those scholarships. Each year I receive an Endowment Report on the growth of those funds that offer scholarships and look forward to knowing which students have benefited the previous year from funding. My goal is to inspire others to help fund or add to existing UMW Scholarships. In

2023, I funded another scholarship in memory of my mother for students preparing for a career in education.

13. <u>THE PANDEMIC OF 2020</u>

How the world changed! I had planned trips to Italy, Mexico, and Greece. Instead, life consisted of reading, virtual yoga classes, and classes on COVID-19 from the UMW. Those classes were excellent, and inspired me to fund the Perkins Research Scholarship immediately.

The Pandemic offered me the opportunity to reflect on my life, education and how I might make a difference. I was no longer willing to travel as before. How could I help? By using my voice in my local community, at my university, on public radio, and the power of messaging because of my training in infectious diseases.

Dealing with a virus that has a high morbidity rate wasn't new to me, during the AIDS epidemic of the 1980's, I was on the front-line seeing patients in a Free Clinic in D.C. I was in New York City in January, on a cruise ship in February and skiing in Sun Valley, Idaho on March 5, 2020. These were three epicenters for

COVID-19 in the United States. Then suddenly - BAM - I was home alone for months. What was day-to-day life like during those months? To say the least, the skies were a more vivid blue and the air less polluted with less travel.

At times I found the year both depressing and anxious. It was especially difficult for those at highest risk: the elderly (a category in which I found myself), front line workers (like my family), minorities, and low-income households. Frustrated and depressed with the loss of any hope of European travel, I found myself home alone and found some days lonely and depressing with distance from both family and friends. The Pandemic offered us a new way to appreciate and enjoy life with family. Since an outside visit was possible with social distancing, those were some of the best visits in years. We lived with less and appreciated more. Even from family, routine hugs and cheek to cheek kisses were no longer an option. We stood in the driveway and blew kisses! Jack and Karen

were my superheroes during the Pandemic.
They are both physicians who treated COVID
patients, home schooled their three children
and provided a safe and balanced life during the
Pandemic.

I worked out with my trainer in my driveway,
and enjoyed zoom yoga and classes from my
university. I read incredible books as well. One
was titled *The Immortal Life of Henriette Lacks*.
It is the story of a black woman with cancer
treated at Johns Hopkins, whose name was
released. Her cancer cells were taken for
research both without her knowledge or
consent. Both today, considered unethical and
like other trials on blacks resulted in distrust of
the medical community. Her story reminded
me that while I was doing my animal research at
the NIH enjoying black tie dinners at Johns
Hopkins, I was clueless to the ethical issues of
other researchers and unethical practices. It
was not until I became a medical officer at the
FDA that I became knowledgeable on clinical

trials. I devoted my career to protecting the rights of subjects and patients in research trials. I audited trials and spoke at universities and medical societies around the world on the necessity of properly consenting those in trials. I audited study data to assure meaningful data was collected. If not, those in trials were potentially at risk without any hope of benefit from the research.

14. <u>TEACHING YOGA</u>

While working in the Washington area, I was introduced to Iyengar yoga. I had taken yoga in California and was not a fan. However, this form of yoga appealed to me as it is medically based and often used as an alternative for Western medical therapy.   In fact, there are NIH studies that have shown that it can be effective.

It is alignment based and I believed it was less likely to cause me more injuries after my skiing adventures. Cal, my husband, was given Iyengar yoga as a prescription for one of his therapies to aid in balance.

Yoga has enhanced my life by bringing balance into my world of working and family. In class we were always taught to practice at home. I confess I rarely did until Cal became so weak with cancer. Then, I became an avid practitioner. My classmates said, "Jerri, you are getting really good!" Yes, if you practice you do improve.

When I moved to South Carolina after Cal's death, I could not find a local Iyengar studio. My trainer suggested I become certified in yoga and teach. Teaching yoga was not my goal, but I said yes. I just wanted to be a student. What I found was teaching makes me a better student. I love sharing what I have learned! My students have said, "I sleep better, I can climb more without becoming breathless." What a great feeling to know you have made a difference.

Devon, my granddaughter, said I was her "hero" for standing on my head. The kids love seeing their grandmother doing her headstand!

I became involved with exercise primarily due to an injury that happened while skiing with Cal. However, when I was a student, females were given minimum requirements and less opportunities in sports than men. My focus was always academic. This changed when I first skied with Cal - he was an expert skier from childhood - on rental skies, on the last run of the day in Heavenly Valley and I was racing to keep up. My knee took the hit, and I was in a cast for 6 weeks and eventually had surgery. After physical therapy and being determined to continue skiing with Cal, I found my first trainer, Nancy. My total focus was on my lower body. Being a good trainer, she said yes but insisted I also work on my upper body. Thank you, Nancy! For years I skied with braces until my muscles were strong enough without them.

The ski accident forced attention to my legs. Having Jack by C-Section brought attention to my abdominal muscles. I went to a studio in DC for core work. When Cal's cancer affected his ability to hoist the sail and operate the winches, again I returned to Nancy. How do I improve my upper body strength? Because of the challenges I faced and how motivated I was to continue, saying yes to exercise has empowered me to walk into any gym with confidence.

15. <u>WHY WRITE THIS BOOK?</u>

"If you can dream it, you can do it." - *Walt Disney*

I want a better world with freedom for women and children. I love the intellectual challenge of science and learning! If I could give but one gift to the world it would be my quest for knowledge! The more I know, the more I realize I don't know. In the words of Socrates, "I know only one thing: that I know nothing."

Hopefully, the scholarships at the University will benefit others in their quest for knowledge and enhance their lives. If you are blessed to have done well with the education provided you, I believe you have an obligation to pay it forward. In the inspiring words of Lynn Twist, "it's not how much wealth you accumulate, it's how you allocate."

I wish I could educate more but I can educate some; one at a time.

While on one of my travels, I met two authors who wrote a book with proceeds for Scholarships to their University and this inspired me. I believe what they did was meaningful. I look forward to another challenge to help students accomplish their educational goals.

I would be very happy if this book inspires others to achieve more and grow more than they imagined. I have learned much on this new adventure of writing, publishing and fund raising but also having fun working with friends and my University on making this possible. I know firsthand that sharing your stories with others is inspiring.

Will I succeed? I am told the odds are against it. While I have written several Christmas books for my grandchildren, that does not make me a writer and certainly not a known one.

"The greater danger for most of us is not that our aim is too high and we miss it, but that it is too low and we reach it." - *Michelangelo*

There are some things I had to think about before taking on this new challenge. I know that I am confident I can self-publish. I have an editor from my previous books given to my family members. And I am very passionate about my mission. I definitely believe in myself and have invested in writing and publishing this book for the benefit of women, education, and my university. As Robert Keefe once said, "I truly believe that the more education we have, the better society is, the more tolerant people are. With education, there's no problem that can't be solved."

Will this be enough to bring success? Only my readers can answer this question, but I have always been an optimist!

With passion, perseverance, and determination I have already succeeded by writing the book.

In so doing, it has given me purpose to wake up in the morning and look forward to sharing stories. When consulting, I would get up, go to my office, and say to myself, "they pay me to do what I love, I would do it for free!" And this one I'm doing for love!

Hopefully my stories will inspire students and Alumni particularly females, to reach beyond their dreams, say yes to challenges that seem beyond your grasp and accept life's challenges. Say yes to a successful life!

16. <u>ACKNOWLEDGEMENTS</u>

This book would not be possible without my Editor, AJ — without her help, I would not have attempted this challenge! It's just so much better with her aid and together we brought it to a totally new level.

Mary Beth and Nicholas Claps book, *Lessons and Suggestions for Building your Wealth*. All profits go to their University and that inspired me to write this book with profits going to my University, Mary Washington in Virginia.

University of Mary Washington for their support during my years without the love of my life, Cal, John Calvin Perkins, who has many scholarships in his memory.

And the support of family and friends, who helped on my journey writing this book.

Dr. Jack Perkins, Carolyn Meagher, Betty Spencer, Stacey Saritelli, Peggy Parker, Maggie

Rhoades, Dr. Lou Ann Eader, Dr. Alison Martin, Nancy McCarthy and Dr. Crystal Caudle.

All proceeds from this book will go directly to the University of Mary Washington for funding future scholarships.

17. <u>SCHOLARSHIPS: REMEMBERING CAL AND MOTHER</u>

John C. and Jerri Barden Perkins '61 Study Abroad Scholarship

Dr. Perkins created this scholarship with a gift in 2013 to support students with demonstrated financial need participating in semester or year-long education abroad experiences.

Highlights:

- Four students spent their spring semester studying at the University of Deusto, Bilbao, Spain:
    - French and Spanish major, international affairs minor, spring 2016
    - Business administration major, spring 2017
    - Sociology/practical ethics major, spring 2018

- o Economics and sports management major, spring 2019

- When COVID cancelled international travel, a student studied at the Akita University, Japan, completely online.
  - o International business major, spring 2020

Notes from students:

- I am so grateful to have received this scholarship because it gives me more confidence in myself to study abroad and continue to work hard to reach my dreams. Being able to say that I was chosen for this scholarship is wonderful and it feels amazing to know I have people helping me along my journey.

- I chose the Business and Global Studies Program at the University of Deusto to grow as a student and an individual. This program expanded my knowledge of Economics and Business by allowing me to learn the subject in another country

(Spain) and understand the fundamentals of international economies. I learned a significant amount about business and the impact of international funding on communities. In particular, I am now more interested in possibly working with the International Monetary Fund or with an organization that partners with them.

Graduate Updates:

- The student who studied with Akita University is working in globalization and public relations in Aichi, Japan.
- The business administration major became a Business Analyst with Fannie Mae.
- The sociology/practical ethics major earned a Master of Social Work from Virginia Commonwealth University and is employed as a Mental Health Clinician. She interned at Safe Harbor and was a Justice and Advocacy Fellow with Just Neighbors.

John C. and Jerri Barden Perkins '61 Classics, Philosophy, and Religion Research Endowment

Dr. Perkins funded this endowment in 2019 to support majors in the Department of Classics, Philosophy, and Religion conduct on-site research at archaeological digs, cultural heritage sites, research institutions, and museums. The University may also use the endowment to facilitate the loan or acquisition of objects for exhibition and study on campus.

Highlights:

> Although the endowment had not produced an award budget yet in 2019, when Dr. Perkins learned that a student needed help to participate in a trip to Nepal, she gave an additional gift to help the student. The student, a historic preservation major and museum studies minor, participated in the faculty-led "International Perspectives and Civic Engagement" course in Nepal over the winter break of 2019-20.

- For 2020-21 the endowment supported a Latin and art history major with her honors research. The student was a spring 2021 Humanities in Action Intern with the Greater Fredericksburg Habitat for Humanity and an intern with the Chrysler Museum of Art summer 2021.

- The endowment helped two students, a Latin major museum studies minor, and a classical civilization and historic preservation major participate in "UMW in Rome, Latin Inscriptions & the Eternal City" summer 2022.

- A classical civilization and historic preservation major received funding to participate in the Monticello-UVA Archaeological Field School in 2021-22.

- A classical archaeology major received funding to participate in Archaeological Techniques and Center Research

(Archaeo Tek Canada) in Transylvania Romania, summer 2022.

- A classical archaeology major museum studies minor received funding to participate in the Dzhungar Mountains Archeology Project (Kazakhstan), summer 2023.

Graduate Updates:

- The student who traveled to Nepal graduated Phi Beta Kappa and summa cum laude in 2022 and took a job with the National Defense University Library.

- The Latin and art history major graduated Phi Beta Kappa and summa cum laude in 2022 and was the recipient of the Melchers Award for Excellence in Art History, Barbara Leigh Gregg Prize for Excellence in Greek, and the Laura V. Sumner Award for Excellence in Classics. She is currently a Ph.D. student at Duke University.

- The 2021-22 classical civilization and historic preservation major graduated summa cum laude with departmental honors in 2023. In addition, the student won the Laura V. Sumner Award for Excellence in Classics

Jerri Barden Perkins '61 Scholarship

Dr. Perkins funded a scholarship in 2020 to benefit students majoring in one of the physical sciences. To qualify, a student must have demonstrated financial need and a minimum 3.5 GPA in their major field of study.

Highlights:

- The first recipient, a chemistry and business administration major, received the scholarship for 2021-22. In addition, the student worked in the chemistry lab.
- The 2022-23 recipient was a geology and secondary education major.

- A geology, applied physics major received the scholarship for 2023-24. In addition, the student participated in the Summer Science Institute, summer 2023.

Notes from Students:

- Thank you so much for the Jerri Barden Perkins '61 Scholarship! Your kindness allows students like me to freely pursue our future goals and know that there are people that believe we can achieve those goals. I am currently a part time student. I own a cleaning business to help me get through college and I plan to become a travel lab tech once I graduate. It hasn't been an easy journey and It has taken me a while to get to where I am today, but with the help of kind people like you, you make it that much easier. I am truly grateful for the opportunity to attend Mary Washington and I know that I will be able to do great things and return the favor to future students just as you have done to us. Again, thank you so much Jerri and I want you to know that your kindness will have an amazing ripple effect.

- Growing up, I was always told college is what I needed to do, but I never realized until I got to college how financially challenging it would be... My family was kind enough to provide some financial support for college, but I've had to take on many loans to be able to afford going to school... Thankfully, scholarships such as the Jerri Barden Perkins '61 Scholarship have been able to make the financial struggle a little easier. At school has been where I've been able to find people who love and accept me for who I am, and I have found something I am completely passionate about. College has made my love for learning grow, and I am looking forward to sharing what I've learned with future generations.

John C. and Jerri Barden Perkins '61 College of Arts and Sciences Student Research Endowment

Dr. Perkins funded this endowment in memory of her husband, John, in 2021 to support UMW's Summer Science Institute (SSI). SSI is a 10-week summer research program for UMW undergraduates. Students work individually on research projects with dedicated faculty mentors. The University covers the cost of room and board and pays students a stipend. Initially, the endowment will provide a scholarship for the student with the best research presentation and best research poster at the SSI conclusion. As the endowment grows, it will provide overall support for the SSI program and eventually may fund a research team.

Highlights:

- 2021 award winners included an environmental science: natural major and a biology major.

- 2022 award winners included a physics major/math minor, and an environmental science: social major.

Graduate Updates:

- 2021 winners graduated in May 2022 summa cum laude.
- 2022 winners graduated in May 2023, with the environmental science major achieving summa cum laude.

Notes from students:

- Coming to UMW as an environmental science major, I knew I would learn about numerous ways we have an impact on the physical world. I have always wanted to make a difference in understanding how we as a species affect the environment around us. Through my research, I have grown to better understand how the combustion of coal, forming what is commonly known as coal ash, has a negative impact on aquatic ecosystems. Upon completing undergraduate research at UMW, it is my hope that I will continue learning more on environmental issues by attending graduate school and receiving a master's degree in ecotoxicology. It is my personal goal to work for the Environmental Protection Agency, where I hope to be a field scientist that analyzes water quality.

- I have always known that I wanted to be a researcher. The idea of asking a question that might not have an immediate answer excites me. The most exciting part about research is that I get to work towards discovering the answer to my question. I have also always had a passion for animals. I grew up on a farm and animals have always been front and center in my life. Taking care of our animals was the first thing I did in the morning and the last thing I did at night. There is something so genuine about animals that you just do not see with people. People always have a goal or a reason for acting the way they do but animals have no such pretenses. Animals are always the truest forms of themselves, and I take comfort in their consistency.

- The University of Mary Washington has given me an incredible opportunity through the Summer Science Institute where I have been able to further my knowledge of science, research, and the community. Being a physics major, this scholarship has encouraged me to continue with my research on solar powered phone charging stations during the Fall 2022 semester. I have also been inspired to consider careers in the field of research once I have graduated from UMW. This scholarship has not just boosted my morale, but also given me a reward to help further my education, which I am grateful for.

Sybil Sullivan Barden Education Scholarship

Dr. Perkins created this endowment in memory of her mother, Sybil Barden, in 2023 to support students preparing for a career as a public-school teacher. The endowment will produce an award budget for the 2024-25 academic year.

John C. and Jerri Barden Perkins '61 – Washington Scholarship

Dr. Perkins intends to endow a Washington Scholarship through her estate plan. The Washington Scholars program recognizes Virginia high school seniors with exceptional academic credentials and is one of UMW's most prestigious and comprehensive scholarship programs. Washington scholars receive a full-ride merit scholarship for four years of academic study.

About the author

Jerri Barden Perkins, MD

After receiving her medical degree from the Medical College of Virginia, she obtained a Fellowship at the National Institute of Health. While there she found a micro-organism, named for her, *jb strain, M. pulmonis*, which is used as an animal model for research on Rheumatoid Arthritis. From there she became a medical officer at the FDA and an expert on clinical trials. She recommended approval for the first AIDS related therapy. She volunteered in a Free Clinic in Washington D.C. and saw AIDS patients during the epidemic, worked with her community in South Carolina during the Pandemic of 2020 and is actively involved with her alma mater, the University of Mary Washington, where she has funded several scholarships. She opened her Consulting firm in 1984 after leaving the government. She has been recognized by the Association of Clinical

Research Professionals, for her contribution to promoting the value of clinical research.

Her education at Mary Washington College, now the University of Mary Washington, offered her the opportunities and this book is her way of paying it forward.

Made in the USA
Middletown, DE
24 October 2023

41351376R00066